MW01088491

Lexy

Written by K. Davis
Illustrated by Mark Wolfe

Copyright © 2016 Kristi Davis
All rights reserved.
ISBN: 10:1547281294
ISBN: 13: 978-1547281299

This book is dedicated to
Rose

Introduction

Although Lexy is intended for all children, its underlying purpose is to spark joy and ease parents' minds, especially the parents of children with dyslexia. When I first heard that my child had dyslexia, fear lumped in my throat and questions arose: What does this mean? Can it be cured? Will my child ever be able to read? Where do we go for help? I am hoping this book will dispel parents' fears and concerns by letting them know their child is perfect. Trust your child. Recognize his or her strengths, honor them, and rejoice in them!

There are Parent Notes on most pages that put forth indicators and strengths of dyslexia, as well as advice. Most of the advice is from my own experience as a mother of a child with dyslexia and as a reading and spelling tutor. I do not consider myself an expert but simply want to share what I have learned.

What is dyslexia? The International Dyslexia Association (https://dyslexiaida.org/definition-of-dyslexia/) says this: *"Dyslexia is a specific learning disability that is neurobiological in origin. It is characterized by difficulties with accurate and/or fluent word recognition and by poor spelling and decoding abilities. These difficulties typically result from a deficit in the phonological component of language that is often unexpected in relation to other cognitive abilities and the provision of effective classroom instruction. Secondary consequences may include problems in reading comprehension and reduced reading experience that can impede growth of vocabulary and background knowledge."*

I say this: Dyslexia is poor reading skills and even worse spelling despite average or above average intelligence.

Twenty percent of our population has dyslexia, ranging from mild to profound. This condition is not new. Looking back through history, we see that many of our great leaders, inventors, scientists, and artists had dyslexia. What is new is our awareness of it and how to teach these extraordinary people how to read and spell.

In the back of this book, you will find a list of famous people with dyslexia who are paragons of success. There is also a complete list of warning signs from preschool through adulthood contributed by Susan Barton, dyslexia expert and founder of Bright Solutions, which is an organization that provides free unlimited support regarding dyslexia for people around the world. Her website, BrightSolutions.US, has the information you need if you see Lexy as your child.

Lexy displays traits indicative of dyslexia. She is a delightful child, but to learn to read and spell, she will need a system based on the Orton-Gillingham approach. These systems are the only methods scientifically proven to teach people with dyslexia how to read and spell.

Whether or not Lexy reminds you of your child, I hope you and your small wonder revel in who Lexy is and find her to be an inspiration.

K. Davis

Meet Lexy.

She has lots of ideas.

Lexy has ideas about which clothes to wear

Parent Note – Choosing clothing may be one of the earliest signs of your youngster's creative talents. Creativity is not by any means limited to children with dyslexia, but they are often very creative and "out of the box" thinkers.

and which shoes. Lexy likes Velcro more than tying laces.

Parent Note – Difficulty learning to tie shoes is an early indicator of dyslexia. Encourage your child to learn to tie his or her own shoes, but also provide an alternative such as Velcro. This will prevent frustration and promote self-esteem.

Lexy has ideas for Legos.

Parent note – Children with dyslexia are often whole-picture thinkers who possess good 3-D spatial skills. One of the earliest signs of this is the creation of advanced patterns with colors and shapes. Legos easily provide the opportunity for any child, especially one with dyslexia, to express this skill. Let your child have fun creating. Be encouraging, and state what you like about your child's creations.

After building with Legos, Lexy has ideas with crayons.

Parent Note – Coloring is a joyous and creative activity that most children love. Please take notice as your child establishes a dominant hand. Children with dyslexia are often late at this and may even appear to be ambidextrous. Usually, a dominant hand preference is firmly established by four years old.

While Lexy plays with Legos or crayons, she loves to listen to music.

"Please, Mommy, play the Nutcracker again!"

Parent Note – All children should have the opportunity to listen to a variety of music, especially classical, but children with dyslexia may have an even greater appreciation for it. They are often musically gifted.

"A, B, C,
D, E, F, G,
HOW I WONDER
WHAT YOU
ARE,
Q, R, S"

Lexy has ideas about singing "The Alphabet Song"

and "Twinkle, Twinkle, Little Star."

Parent Note – Children with dyslexia are often musically gifted, but memorizing facts or sequences that seem random is usually challenging. Learning the sequence of the alphabet, their address or phone number, days of the week, or months of the year is extremely difficult. For some, it helps to put the facts to the tune of a familiar song. If you Google what you want to memorize, someone may already have put it to music.

Lexy has ideas about helping her mom.

Parent Note – Obviously, supervise for safety, but as often as possible, encourage your child's curiosity. Children with dyslexia often delve deeper with questions of why and how.

Mommy says, "Lexy, what is all of this stuff?"

Lexy tells her mommy, "Those were left over from the sweeper when I

fixed it, but it runs without them."

Parent Note – Dyslexic individuals often have the ability to take things apart, reassemble them, and repair them. They may not even be able to explain it; many just seem to understand innately how things work.

Lexy's ideas prompt lots of questions. "Where does the water come from that pours out of the faucet?"

"How does the washer turn the clothes around like that?"

Parent Note – Take time to answer your child's questions. Show them pictures or YouTube videos, or provide them with hands-on experiences and demonstrations. Pursue an answer as long as it holds their interest. Like Einstein, children with dyslexia and many others are often gifted thinkers and have a love of learning, which will be enhanced by your enthusiasm to explore answers with them. You may learn a few things, too.

At school, Lexy has ideas about spelling and about how to hold her pencil. She grips it tightly. Sometimes the lead crumbles and smudges on her paper, but that's okay. Lexy wipes it all away.

Parent Note – Children with dyslexia often have an unusual pencil grip which can sometimes cause their hand to hurt or cramp. This makes spelling and writing even more difficult. There are a variety of pencil grips on the market that may help. The Ticonderoga Tri-Write pencil, shaped as a triangle, may also be a helpful option. Please note that an unusual pencil grip is a fine motor control skill that can create messy handwriting, known as dysgraphia. Dysgraphia is not unique to dyslexia, but it commonly coexists with it.

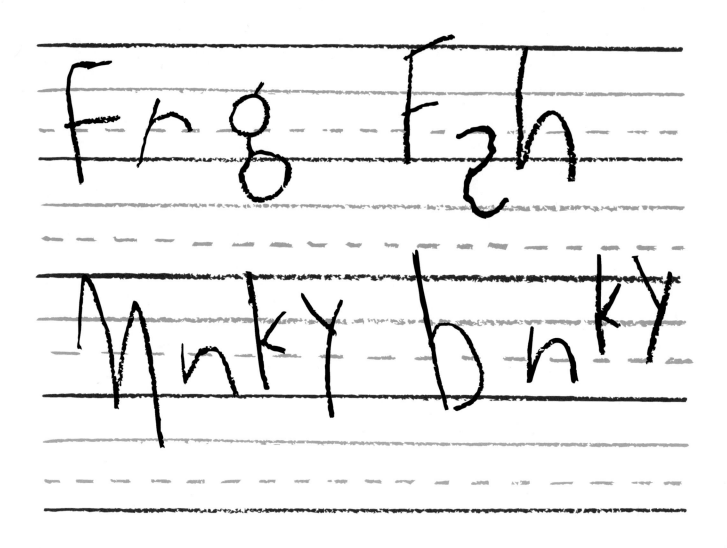

Lexy practices her spelling words every day at home and at school, but during Friday's spelling test, Lexy likes to spell with only consonants…

Parent Note – Poor spelling test performance is not due to the dyslexic child's lack of effort. The child will practice spelling words every day and seem to know them perfectly but then still do poorly on a test the very next day. Also note that it is very typical for a person with dyslexia to omit vowels when spelling, or not to be able to spell those same words a week later.

An Orton-Gillingham based method of instruction is the only scientifically proven method to help reading and spelling skills for dyslexia.

except for silent e. Lexy loves to decorate lots of words with silent e.

Parent Note – Silent e is extremely confusing to dyslexic children. They are not sure why or when it is used. We typically tell them that silent e makes the vowel long, but what about words like "have," "bridge," or "dance"? The Barton Reading & Spelling System, an Orton-Gillingham based approach, dedicates an entire level to silent e. It is one of the longest levels in the entire system, and that's because there are six reasons for silent e.

Story time is Lexy's favorite. Listening to her teacher read gives Lexy lots of ideas about things she might do. Lexy has sailed the seas with Pippi Longstocking, wears a deerstalker hat when doing detective work with Nate the Great, and even has ideas about how to make a model of Niagara Falls with Hank Zipzer.

Parent Note – Audio books allow a dyslexic child to listen to stories at or beyond his or her grade level. Typically, these children hate to read but love to listen to someone else read. So read to your child or offer audio books. School textbooks are also available on audio. Places to investigate for audio books include Learning Ally http://learningally.org, Librivox, https://librivox.org/ with free public domain audio books, your local library's audio books, and audible.com.

3 6 9 12 15

jin gle bells jin gle bells

18 21

jin gle all the way

Lexy has ideas about math, too. She loves to skip count by singing the numbers to the tune of her favorite songs. She sings the three's to the tune of Jingle Bells.

Parent Note – Children with dyslexia often have difficulties with math. They struggle memorizing what seems to be arbitrary facts such as the multiplication tables. Transposing numbers when copying from the board or a book or during the borrow and carry process is very common. Memorizing any sequence of steps is difficult, which can make long division painful to learn. Typically, these children have directional issues (left/right), which makes place value very confusing, especially when decimals are introduced, and the greater than and less than signs can be a nightmare. Here's the blessing: they usually understand the concepts. So, a calculator will get them through basic math facts and allow them to advance to higher levels of math.

Lexy loves to dance the hokey pokey, but she has her
own ideas about that, too.

Parent Note – Left/right confusion is common among children with dyslexia and is worse if they are tired or ill. These children often mix up any directional words, such as before and after, over and under, in front and behind, up and down, north and south, and east and west. There are a variety of ways to teach left and right. Google and select a method to find a way that works for your child.

Lexy has ideas about telling time.

Parent Note – Children with dyslexia often struggle with learning to tell time on a circular clock with hands. They may confuse the concepts of before and after and struggle with the math involved and the terminology of quarters. A plastic handheld clock that your child can manipulate may be the best and least frustrating way to teach these skills. And please, no roman numerals to add to your child's confusion!

After school, Lexy loves to play!

Parent Note – Many children with dyslexia have exceptional eye-hand coordination skills and excel at athletics. Notice the professional athletes in the list of famous people with dyslexia at the back of this book.

When Lexy gets home, she can't wait to talk about her school day. "Mommy, Daddy, look—I won first place at the school art fair!"

Parent Note – Children with dyslexia often have talents in one or several of the arts. Encourage, applaud, and praise!

"And I'm a pilgrim in the Christmas play!"

Parent Note – Especially when children with dyslexia are ill or tired, words get confused. If your child mixes up words or events, praise for the positive with a hug and gently remind him or her of the correct word: "Awesome! But do you mean the Thanksgiving play?" Mention it only once. Children will ask when they need you to clarify.

"Can I learn to play the trombone?"

Parent Note – Despite years of instruction, many children with dyslexia cannot read printed music. However, they are often quite gifted and can play very complicated pieces by ear. So, investigate the Suzuki method of instruction.

Lexy's daddy says, "Whoa! Slow down, and tell us one thing at a time."

Parent Note – Enthusiasm may make anyone blurt out words in excitement. ADD can, too. However, children with ADD are able to learn to read and spell. So do not allow the school or anyone to blame your child's poor reading and spelling skills on ADD. About 40% of children with dyslexia also have ADD. So while the two may coexist, ADD is not the cause of your child's reading and spelling problems.

Lexy notices a familiar smell coming from the kitchen. She has her own ideas about how to say lots of words. "Egg siting! Mommy is making psketties!"

Parent Note – One red flag of dyslexia is mixing up the pronunciation of a word. It is common for very young children to do this, but the child without dyslexia can be taught correct pronunciations usually by kindergarten.

Lexy slurps spaghetti noodles and giggles with her daddy as he tries to teach her the proper way to say "spa-ghet-ti." But she still says "psketties."

Parent Note – Having a little fun together with the mispronunciations is a way to acknowledge them without hurting the child's self-esteem by constant corrections. Know the sensitivities of your child, and only be playful about this if your child can be playful about it, too.

Sometimes, Daddy gets mixed up, and he says, "psketties." They both snort with laughter, and then Lexy teaches Daddy "p-skeh-tees." Mommy giggles with them, too.

Parent Note – Dyslexia is an inherited condition. At least one of the parents will have also struggled with reading and spelling. Both parents should review the Warning Signs at the end of this book. Mixing up sounds and syllables in long words is one of the Warning Signs.

After dinner, Lexy and her mommy take a walk through the woods. Lexy has ideas there, too. "Mommy, why does this tree feel so smooth and this one is rough? And why does this leaf have pointy edges? If I plant this acorn, will we get a big tree in our yard?"

Parent Note – Curiosity about gardening, nature, or any science is something to cultivate. You never know which of these fields may need another expert, and it could very well be your child!

Lexy puts the acorn into her pocket and runs on through the woods.
Her mommy tries to keep up.

"Time to do homework," Daddy says. Lexy has her own ideas about doing homework. She dances about the room and listens as Daddy reads her schoolwork aloud. Then, she sings the answers, and Daddy writes them down for her.

Parent Note – Kinesthetic learners come in all kinds of packages. No matter what type of learner your child is, allowing or incorporating physical interaction often boosts memory and learning. Reading the homework aloud and then taking dictation for your child with dyslexia will speed up the homework process and make it easier on both of you.

It's nighttime now. Lexy takes a bath and puts on her pajamas.
She remembers the acorn. She gets it out of her pocket and lays it on
her nightstand as she climbs into bed.

Lexy looks at her acorn and has ideas about where she will plant it.

Lexy closes her eyes. She dreams colorful dreams, and tomorrow, she will wake with lots of ideas.

Parent Note – Praise, encourage, and love your children. Kiss them. Hug and squeeze them, and never stop saying how much you love them.

From the Author

The character of Lexy is based on my own lovely daughter, Rose. I homeschooled Rose, or rather, she homeschooled me. She taught me about dyslexia and so much more. I can give all of this great advice in the Parent Notes because Rose taught me.

I often stumbled as a parent. Though I am naturally a patient person, I misunderstood her need to think and take longer to process as defiance by not answering me quickly enough. I would lose my patience, and I am sure she sat in the time-out chair way too many times, when in actuality, it should have been me in time-out. Rose was never defiant. She was just thinking. She had her own ideas about everything, and I was often in too much of a hurry to recognize her gifts.

When I found out Rose had dyslexia, I went on a research quest and found an overwhelming amount of information, but it didn't need to be this difficult. I've tried to simplify it with Lexy so that it will not seem so overwhelming for you. Susan Barton's Bright Solutions is the most comprehensive website about dyslexia that I know. It took me a couple of years of searching and experimenting before I found it. I cannot praise Susan Barton enough. She has dedicated her life to, and is truly a champion for, people with dyslexia.

Lexy has dyslexia, but she is someone to whom we can all relate. All of us may have some of the warning signs of dyslexia, but for it to be dyslexia you must have three or more warning signs from the list on page 40. For instance, I have always confused my left and right, but I have no other warning signs. Rose's father has dyslexia, but he never confuses left and right. So not all people with dyslexia will have all of the warning signs, and many people may have one or two of the signs but not have dyslexia. However, if your child is struggling with reading and spelling and displays three or more of the warning signs, it is time to seriously investigate dyslexia.

This is what I have learned: Teach your child to read with a method of instruction based on the Orton-Gillingham approach.

You can do it yourself. It takes time, discipline, and dedication. You can hire a professional, but if they've never heard the words Orton-Gillingham, stay away. Sadly, most teachers and public schools have never heard of Orton-Gillingham. If your school is using such a method, count you and your child blessed.

After putting Rose through so many ineffective reading and spelling programs, the Barton System worked for us. It is not the only Orton-Gillingham system out there, but in my understanding and experience, it is the most organized and easiest to implement.

Susan Barton wrote it so that parents can implement it themselves. That's what I did. It is amazing! Within just a few months, the results I observed with Rose inspired me to teach the Barton System to others, and I became a Barton Tutor certified at the Masters Level.

If your child has dyslexia, whether you decide on Susan Barton's program or another, gather the information she has made available to you for free on her BrightSolutions.US website to help you decide how to enhance your child's life.

This book is dedicated to my daughter, Rose, to my husband, Bob, and to all people, especially those with lots of ideas.

Kristi Davis

About the Artist

A believer in community development and supporting local businesses in Charleston, West Virginia, Mark Wolfe has invested expertise and time into helping others improve their lives. His company, Mark Wolfe Design (MWD) has won several regional and state-wide awards, including 2008 West Virginia Main Street Business Person of the Year and 2012 Charleston East End Main Street Volunteer of the Year.

After nine years with both niche and prestige advertising and design firms, Mark started his own firm, Mark Wolfe Design, and has been a successful entrepreneur ever since. MWD celebrate its 23rd year in business July, 2017. Mark credits his success as the result of client loyalty, and many clients return to MWD for customized, clean, contemporary and original designs and faithful service to each client's needs. Mark's clients are from national to regional small and large companies and organizations.

MWD specializes in Corporate Identity, Social Media, Web Design, Photography and helping to establish smaller companies with a strong marketing and design experience. MWD is fully equipped to work in all mediums; Video, Web and Print.

Mark has been illustrating all his life and this book is cited as one of his favorite projects.

Warning Signs of Dyslexia

If a child has 3 or more of the following warning signs, encourage that child's parents and teachers to learn more about dyslexia.

In Preschool

- delayed speech
- mixing up the sounds and syllables in long words
- chronic ear infections
- stuttering
- constant confusion of left versus right
- late establishing a dominant hand
- difficulty learning to tie shoes
- trouble memorizing their address, phone number, or the alphabet
- can't create words that rhyme
- a close relative with dyslexia

In Elementary School

- dysgraphia (slow, non-automatic handwriting that is difficult to read)
- letter or number reversals continuing past the end of first grade
- extreme difficulty learning cursive
- slow, choppy, inaccurate reading:
  - guesses based on shape or context
  - skips or misreads prepositions (at, to, of)
  - ignores suffixes
  - can't sound out unknown words
- terrible spelling
- often can't remember sight words (they, were, does) or homonyms (their, they're, and there)
- difficulty telling time with a clock with hands
- trouble with math
  - memorizing multiplication tables
  - memorizing a sequence of steps
  - directionality
- when speaking, difficulty finding the correct word
  - lots of "whatyamacallits" and "thingies"
  - common sayings come out slightly twisted
- extremely messy bedroom, backpack, and desk
- dreads going to school
  - complains of stomach aches or headaches
  - may have nightmares about school

In High School

All of the above symptoms plus:

- limited vocabulary
- extremely poor written expression
  - large discrepancy between verbal skills and written compositions
- unable to master a foreign language
- difficulty reading printed music
- poor grades in many classes
- may drop out of high school

In Adults

Education history similar to above, plus:

- slow reader
- may have to read a page 2 or 3 times to understand it
- terrible speller
- difficulty putting thoughts onto paper
  - dreads writing memos or letters
- still has difficulty with right versus left
- often gets lost, even in a familiar city
- sometimes confuses b and d, especially when tired or sick

To Learn More:

Attend our workshops

Call for free e-newsletter

Visit our website

Order our videos

Bright Solutions for Dyslexia
Email: info@BrightSolutions.US
(408) 559-3652
www.BrightSolutions.US

Famous People With Dyslexia

Source: https://en.wikipedia.org/wiki/List_of_people_diagnosed_with_dyslexia

Sam Allardyce, English footballer and football manager

Anthony Andrews, English actor

Jennifer Anniston, actress

Louise Arnold, English author

Michael "Atters" Attree, English satirical writer and comedian

Abhishek Bachchan, Indian actor and producer

Geoff Barrow, English musician

Princess Beatrice of York, member of British Royal Family

Alexander Graham Bell, inventor and scientist

Michael Bennet, United States Senator from Colorado

Gavin Newsom, Mayor of San Francisco, Lieutenant Governor of California

Robert Benton, screenwriter and film director

Orlando Bloom, actor

Roberto Bolano, Chilean novelist and poet

Jeremy Bonderman, baseball player

Lara Flynn Boyle, American actress

Richard Branson, entrepreneur

Chrisann Brennan, an American Artist and the author of The Bite in the Apple

Marcus Brigstocke, English comedian and satirist

Erin Brockovich, legal clerk, socio-environmental activist

Max Brooks, author, screenwriter, son of actress Anne Bancroft and director Mel Brooks

Neil Bush, businessman and son of George H. W. Bush

Octavia Butler, science fiction author

Celine Byrne, soprano

Stephen J. Cannell, creator of shows such as The A-Team

Lewis Carroll, author and mathmetician

Gary Cohn, COO of Goldman Sachs

Charles "Pete" Conrad Jr., astronaut and third man to walk on the moon

Carl XVI Gustaf, king of Sweden

Carl Philip of Sweden, prince of Sweden

Dave Chalk, Canadian broadcaster and technology journalist

John Chambers, CEO of Cisco

Cher, singer and actress, and Chaz Bono (formerly known as Chastity)

Amy Childs, model and reality television personality

Timothy Clifford, British art historian

Jason Conley, American Basketball player

Anderson Cooper, American journalist

Tom Cruise, actor

Pierre Curie, scientist

Leonardo da Vinci, painter and polymath

Clark Janell Davis, Miss Kentucky 2015

John de Lancie, actor

Samuel R. Delany, science fiction author and literary critic

Paul Dewar, Canadian MP from 2006 – 2015

Patrick Dempsey, actor

Andrew Dorneburg, award-winning author and chef

Michael Dudikoff, actor

Arjan Ederveen, Dutch actor and comedian

Thomas Edison, inventor

Albert Einstein, scientist

Fae Ellington, OD, Jamaican media personality and lecturer

Nelsan Ellis, actor

Paloma Faith, Singer-songwriter and actress

Alexander Faludy, youngest Cambridge undergraduate for 200 years

Michael Faraday, scientist

Trevor Ferrell, advocate for the homeless

Steve Fielding, Australian politician

Fannie Flagg, comedian and author

Ben Fogle, English television presenter

Richard Ford, author

Paul Frappier, musician and hip hop MC

Galileo Galilei, scientist

Noel Gallagher, musician

Karina Galvez, Ecuadorian-American poet, TV and radio personality

Whoopi Goldberg, American actress, comedian, TV personality

Alison Goldfrapp, English musician

Terry Goodkind, American writer

Frank Gore, American football player

Mike Gravel, former United States Senator from Alaska

Brian Grazer, producer

Jerry Hall, model

Susan Hampshire, actress

Salma Hayek, actress

Mark Henry, professional wrestler

John Hickenlooper, Governor of Colorado

Jack Horner, paleontologist

Anthony Hopkins, actor

John Irving, novelist

Caitlyn Jenner, Olympic athlete

Steve Jobs, co-founder of Apple Inc.

John Ive, Chief Design Office for Apple Inc.

Ingvar Kamprad, Industrialist, founder of IKEA

Dean Kamen, inventor, Segway human transport, Luke arm, FIRST Lego League

Rebecca Kamen, artist and sculptor

Paul Kanjorski, former Member of the U.S. House of Representatives from Pennsylvania

Cath Kidston, designer and businesswoman

Mollie King, singer and songwriter

Laura Kirkpatrick, model

Keira Knightley, actress

Willem Johan Kolff, physician

David Koresh, leader of the Branch Davidians

J.F. Lawton, writer, producer, and director

Angie Le Mar, comedian

Peter Leitch, New Zealand businessman and philanthropist

Jay Leno, talk show host and comedian

Tom Lewis, golfer

Kenny Logan, rugby player

Greg Loufanis, Olympic diver

Louis of Luxembourg, prince of Luxembourg

Dan Malloy, Governor of Connecticut

James Clerk Maxwell, scientist

Mireille Mathieu, French singer

Charlotte McKinney, model and actress

Steve McQueen, artist and film director

Kendrick Meek, former Member of the U.S. House of Representatives from Florida

James William Middleton, brother of Catherine, Duchess of Cambridge

Mika, singer-songwriter

Alyssa Milano, American actress

Lorin Morgan-Richards, author and illustrator, publisher of Celtic Family Magazine

Dorit Moussaieff, First Lady of Iceland

Shlomo Moussaieff, jewelry businessman and Bible expert

Don Mullan, Irish author, producer and humanitarian

Jamie Murray, English actress

Roísin Murphy, Irish singer

Steven Naismith, Scottish footballer

Fred Newman, actor, sound engineer, producer, author

Gavin Newsom, Lt Governor of California

Jace Norman, American Actor

Paul Oakenfold, a record producer and trance DJ

Olav V of Noway, reign 1957 – 1991

Jamie Oliver, chef and television host

Paul Orfalea, founder of FedEx Kinko's

Ozzy Osbourne, musician

Brendan O'Carroll, Irish actor

Diamond Dallas Page (Page Falkinburg), professional wrestler, actor and author

Theo Paphitis, businessman, panelist on Dragons' Den

Tom Pellereau, inventor

Pablo Picasso, Spanish artist, sculptor

Daniel Powter, singer and songwriter

Hal Prewitt, Artist, photographer, entrepreneur and racecar driver

Scott Quinnell, rugby player

Bodo Ramelow, Minister-President of Thuringia

Robert Rauschenberg, American artist

Keanu Reeves, actor

Nicholas Winding Refn, film director

Iwan Rheon, Welsh actor and singer/songwriter

Guy Ritchie, film director

David Rockefeller, American business executive and philanthropist

Richard Rogers, architect

Louis Rosenberg, American Entrepreneur, author, screenwriter, inventor and professor

Lee Ryan, singer and songwriter

Rex Ryan, head coach, Buffalo Bills

Mark Schlereth, American football player

Charles Schwab, founder of U.S. brokerage firm

Tim Scott, guitarist

Jo Self, artist

Peter Shumlin, Governor of Vermont

Bryan Singer, film director

John Skoyles, neuroscientist and evolutionary psychologist

Neil Smith, American football player

Steven Spielberg, film director

Jackie Stewart, Scottish racing driver

Joss Stone, singer

Helen B. Taussig, cardiologist

Tim Tebow, American football player

Nikola Tesla, scientist and engineer

Bella Thorne, American actress

Kara Tointon, English actress

Jules Verne, French author

Victoria, Crown Princess of Sweden, heir-apparent to the Swedish throne

Lindsay Wagner, actress

Butch Walker, singer and record producer

Ben Way, entrepreneur

Ben Weir, guitarist

Florence Welch, English musician

Mark Wilkinson, furniture designer

Toyah Wilcox, actress and singer

Roger Ross Williams, Oscar-winning director and producer

Holly Willoughby, television presenter

Henry Winkler, actor, spokesman for the Dyslexia Foundation

Joshua Wong Chi-fung, an activist and a protester from Hong Kong

Lee Kuan Yew, first Prime Minister of Singapore

Channing Tatum, actor and model

Benjamin Zephaniah, poet

For a list of over 200 famous people who have dyslexia organized by profession

go to: http://www.dys-add.com/dyslexia.html#anchorFamousLists

Acknowledgments

Susan Barton

for changing our lives: my daughter's, my own, and one creative person at a time. Also, this book could not serve its purpose without her expert advice, suggestions, and support.
BrightSolutions.US

Mark Wolfe

for understanding the importance of my Lexy mission and for not only breathing life into my treasured little character, but for giving me joy as you created her.
MarkWolfeDesign.com

Scott Oney

my editor, whom I trust and adore. You are prompt, precise, and encouraging. I can't imagine writing a book without you.

Dr. Don Blackburn

for being the person to bring dyslexia to my attention and for supporting Rose and me on our journey. And thank you for improving Rose's coordination and focusing ability, which lessened her headaches and ultimately improved her stamina for learning. It was always fun to see you and your compassionate staff.
DevisionAcademy.com
COVD.org

HSLDA

for supporting homeschoolers everywhere and for having a compassionate, helpful and knowledgeable Special Needs staff.
Hslda.org/strugglinglearner/

Reading Assist Institute

located in Wilmington, Delaware, for serving children of Delaware with an Orton-Gillingham based approach to reading and spelling and for offering free training to anyone willing to volunteer for a couple of hours a week to tutor reading and spelling for one full school year.
ReadingAssist.org

Math-U-See
Steve Demme

for inspiring our skip counting to music. We did it a little differently but still used Jingle Bells for the three's. Thank you!
MathUsee.com

Robert Davis

my husband, for helping me appreciate thinking in pictures instead of words and also for helping me understand the painful and yet miraculous compensation techniques he used to read and comprehend, since no one throughout his educational life recognized his dyslexia.

And to Rose, for enriching my life and making all of this possible.

52417981R00027

Made in the USA
San Bernardino, CA
19 August 2017